THE
ROAD
BETWEEN

THE
ROAD
BETWEEN

Courtney Peppernell

Andrews McMeel
PUBLISHING®

For MaMa

Acknowledgments

I have loved working on this poetry collection. The publication and creative process would not be possible without the involvement of the following people and organizations: James De'Bono, Emma Batting, Andrews McMeel Publishing, Kirsty Melville, Patty Rice, and Ryan Gerber for his artwork. I would also like to thank my support system: my family for their unconditional support; my dog, Hero, for keeping my feet warm while I write; and my partner, Rhian. It would be an honor to walk every road with you.

Twitter: @CourtPeppernell
Instagram: @itsonlyyforever
Email: courtney@pepperbooks.org

The road between is the road you take
from losing yourself to finding yourself

As you go on your way
with one foot in front of the other
you'll see all sorts of things
Maybe some mountains
a handful of sunsets
maybe even a shooting star
or a raging storm
You will have moments
where you might feel alone
and spend days and nights
just wanting to come home
But for all the adventures that you seek
and the roads between
just remember to follow your footsteps
each day
week by week

THE
CAVE

When you are sad and your troubles are too much
a cave inside your heart opens and asks you inside
And in you go with your hopes and your dreams
wanting to find solace without breaking at your seams
And if the walls were made of cotton and kept you safe
I'd say stay inside this cave, away from life—just in case
But I would be lying, because the cave is a temporary fix
So when you are ready, you must come back to the light
and love the day as much as you love the night

Even if you cannot see the pain
    it still exists
A tree can be tall with pretty leaves
but underneath the soil
    the roots are dying

Things that make me Sad

Not everyone has a home
Children are still victims of war
Gay is still used as an insult
Some people don't live to see
things get better
Some women are scared
to walk the streets alone
Some people of color too
There is all this money in the world
but poverty exists
Some leaders are so selfish
they do what's best for themselves
and not for the world

It feels like my life is just passing by,
gone with the current and the wind
And I'm fighting for my right
to continue asking why
things happen and people always leave,
and I'm left to sit under the sky
thinking about the things I've lost
and all the things I want to achieve

But sometimes people just need space
It's nothing personal
You just need to let them be

It was five o'clock
in the morning
and I couldn't sleep
So I drew a breath
and released a sigh
wondering
how things would get better
if I had forgotten
how to cry

When they told you how much they were suffering,
you responded by holding out your hand
But sometimes pain weighs too much
And worse than being too heavy to carry,
it's contagious

It doesn't matter what you look like
if you love
                they, her, or him
It doesn't matter where you are from
or the color of your skin

Your heart will still break the same way

But how can I escape you
when every song on the radio
reminds me of us
and everything you promised
we would be?

They say shots of whiskey can cure heartache
But the burn isn't as agonizing
as standing in my bedroom
        alone
looking at all the empty spaces
your belongings once filled

We met when we were seventeen at a party across the street, and I remember you were the prettiest girl I'd ever seen. We started dating in May. Our small-town love, it was ours no matter what anyone had to say. We used to camp out in my truck and hang out at the coffee shop, drive-in movies on Saturdays, and I never wanted it to end. I never wanted us to stop. But it was raining one afternoon, late in September, and I said things I didn't mean. So you ended our small-town love, and I just wanted to go back to the moment we met and were only seventeen. And then years went by and we didn't see each other or share any words, and I moved away to the city where all the skyscrapers are and you can't hear the birds. Until one day I went back to our small town and we saw each other in the old coffee shop. You smiled at me and asked me how I'd been. And I wanted to tell you about all the times I kept my feelings to myself, but it was too late because you looked at me and said, "My heart belongs to someone else."

I am still looking for the parts of you that don't exist anymore

It is a lonely emptiness when you watch as they love someone else
It will eat away at you until the day comes when you realize
       you need to move on
because they've been living their life without you

Sometimes it's not even how sad you are after they've gone. It's knowing that all the things you did together, you'll now do alone.

I knew you were leaving
It was never the arguing
or the fading I love yous

It was the way you looked at me
like you were tired
and we were never meant to be

You took every breath,
and I struggle with what is left.
I call it love but my friends call it despair.
And while I'm asking what is and isn't fair,
you've been moving on,
like you just don't care.

You don't get to spend all that time learning someone
only to bring them undone
with all the knowledge you have gained

I've been trying to come up with all these ways to describe what heartbreak feels like. But maybe it's as simple as the knot in my stomach every time I hear the door close.

It reminds me of when you left.

But it rarely happens all at once. Instead the ache takes its time, folding over every memory, reminding you of how things used to be. One minute you are looking at the empty space in the closet and the next you can't watch a movie because it reminds you of your first date together. So you move through each day, hoping the next will bring new strength and you won't think about the way things used to be. Until eventually they have been gone for so long it won't matter. At least not until the night you open their old playlist and it's empty.

All the things I had
your sweater
your shirt
your heart
I returned to you
But I am still
waiting
searching for the parts of me
you stole

It was real in those moments you thought would be forever.
But a heartbreak later and more tears than you ever imagined,
suddenly you are trying to convince yourself it never happened.

It's over
And what keeps me up all night
is not the moment
you closed the door
But realizing that now
we'll never know for sure

If I were brave, I would have handed you the love letters I wrote back in June. But I was afraid and summer ended and you left far too soon. So now I'll never have that dance because I missed all my chances to tell you how I really feel. You are all that I could ever want, and every passing day I wish I could find the words to convince you to come back. Because I'm standing on the edge of a breath, wondering how to reach all that we were before. But all the letters disappeared the day you walked out my door.

It's late and you keep asking for me back
Because you think you still love me.
If you're lonely and want someone to think about
Think about someone else.

In the moments I am alone and I have run out of things to fill my day, I think about all the parts of me you took away. I think about how easily you walked in and made a mess.
I think about how my heart exploded the day you left.

Forgive

Forgive even when you made a mistake
Forgive even when you blamed yourself
Forgive even on the days you stayed in bed
Forgive all the lies you put inside your head
Forgive the weeks when you felt you couldn't go on
Forgive the illness, because you haven't done anything wrong

When you are young, people try to tell you that you haven't lived on this earth long enough to feel the things you do. But butterflies only live for a moment, and I imagine a world of excitement and heartache lived from the instant they spread their wings.

Life isn't always about being in control. I knew a girl who lost herself once. She went so far into the woods I didn't think she would find the light to return. But sometimes people just need to stay in the darkness for a while. It's okay to be sad and quiet. The most important thing you can give to yourself is understanding that in these moments you are still you. Even in the middle of the woods, you are still brave and made from all that is gentle and good.

Your soul is a home
and when it aches
you need to dust
all its parts
and remind your heart
to try again

When you cannot breathe and the walls are crashing down around you, sit quietly, talk slow and soft. Tell yourself the things you would tell someone you love.

I know it is easy for me to tell you that you are wanted and needed. It is easy for me to say that you are important. But this is why I say it. Because you are not a burden. You are not a darkness that no person wants to love. You are the lighthouse on top of the hill, warm and beautiful. A heart, guiding people home.

The ache that sits between your rib cage, it will renew you.
Ache now, love later.

When you are happy, it's easy to say that all things take time and to enjoy life in every moment. It's very different for people who are sad or anxious or living each day feeling like they might not make it to the next. But for the latter of the two, I hope you know that if you keep listening to the positives, eventually they'll come your way too.

It's winter and I'm sitting by the fire under a dark night. And the cloud cover is thick, hiding all the stars. I'm thinking about this house and how a person I don't recognize once called it home. But all the pieces are overwhelming and the thoughts feel too heavy. So I stare at the flames and pray the light won't run away. All these tiny embers, drifting up to the sky, making me believe I will find my way home, back to who I was before each breakdown, and all the reasons to cry. These memories, shared with night and day, and I know that spring will come. Forward from the cave, there is much healing to be done.

THE
CLOSET

You don't need to edit the pronouns
because you are afraid
of what people will think
I will stand with you
There is importance
in your spilled ink

You're standing in front of a beautiful girl
and you're trying to convince her to give you a chance
You're standing in front of a beautiful girl and she's scared
because other girls have broken her heart
      And you're trying to prove you are not like the rest
that you just want to eat takeout and sit in her car
and wear her t-shirts
You're standing in front of a beautiful girl and you know
      she's been hurt
So be gentle with her and be kind to her soul
You're standing in front of a beautiful girl and you know
      her secret
Her heart is not made of snow

Kissing Her

She reminds me of a small town in southern France, full of sweet and beautiful vineyards. Her hair the color of poppies in bloom, her voice the sound of waking up at noon. I could tell you that strangers kiss and it's all the same. But if your heart isn't racing and your words don't fall over each other when you speak, then she is not the one you should be kissing.

I'm jealous of the sheets that hold you while you sleep
and the arms around you
They make me cry
even in the daylight.
I'm jealous of the way he makes you laugh
and how you dress up for him
I'm jealous that his love for you
will never be considered a sin.
I wish all this love I have for you
could be returned
I wish there weren't all this tolerance
still yet to be learned.
I'm jealous of the way he has your heart
because I never had a chance
      not even from the start

I am afraid because if we tell the world
what if our love vanishes
If we tell the world
I am afraid you will go and leave behind
      your scent
      your laugh
      your soul

It feels like you are always waiting
in darkness that doesn't seem fair
and it hurts
It hurts more than anything in your life
You just want to be with her
but the love feels broken
You fight to be together
You fight to love each other
and most days you don't know what to say
because the world wants you both
to be some other way
So the phone stops ringing
and she doesn't come around anymore
Your sweater loses her smell
and her perfume isn't on your sheets
But you want to wait
You want to hold on

It's the goodbyes that stay with us. That morning the cab pulled up outside the airport. You were running late for your flight and I remember the bags at your feet while you paused on the curb to catch your breath. Knowing another seven months had crept up to rest between us, I started to cry. You told me it would be okay. That we had calls and texts and I love yous. But sometimes the distance is too much. And before you could turn and walk away, I kissed you, hoping it would be enough to make you stay.

She wanted to say something. To tell you about the things inside her heart and her mind. But she kept it all a secret, watched as life went by. She slept and dreamt of your lips, she sat and stared at the wall. She counted all the days she leapt forward and all the ones she'd fall. The world kept going, the buzz of the traffic outside, and she stayed in the closet until all the parts of her died.

It's because you never told her
how her soul made the seasons change
So now you see her by the escalators
and she's in the arms of someone else
It's because you made her wait
all those nights you were out
kissing other girls
who never made your heart race
It's because you hurt her
more than anyone ever should
So she let go of all the tears
and kept moving on
while you stayed out late
and made plans that fell through
It's because you forgot what you had
and now she's happier without you

Your chest is bound so tightly
sometimes it's hard to breathe
And every day you think about
the people who don't understand
and the ones who leave
But I hope in time you realize
all those pieces that seem broken
will come back together again
You are a kaleidoscope
of colors that deserve more
Keep holding on
You will survive this war

While they call it "re-invent"
I call it coming home

"I have a daughter," she says
But this is not true
for she is blind to compassion
and cannot let go
of the things she knew
And her words ache
a mother holding a gun
For she has no daughter
       only a son

There was a moment between us when I wanted to lean in and kiss you. But I wasn't sure if you liked women too. So instead I counted the freckles across your nose, hoping you'd want to kiss me back. I held my breath and said a prayer as you leaned in and lost your fingers in my hair. And suddenly this moment between us became a memory for always. Because for every time my heart chose to skip, you were breathing your name into my lips.

It was unexpected love
one that didn't need to be named
it just needed heart

It's when her hand is laced with hers
she feels infinite
Like she can do anything
with a woman by her side

I am no stranger to writing how I feel on paper
and talking about habits of the people I love
and how it makes me soft
wearing my heart on my sleeve
But even though I have loved before
I have never loved in the way I love her
because she makes writing
both simple and complex
She makes my heart
both race and still
She is a hurricane
and sunlight through my windowsill

In another life
I'll reach for her hand
and no one will wonder
if we're friends or something more
In another life
I'll kiss her in the streets
to our favorite song
and no one will look at us
like we're doing something wrong

All this pressure
to be a certain way
turns you into a shell
Forgotten
Hidden
Lost
a prisoner in a cell
Mercy
is to be allowed to go free

Do you remember when you were five years old and you learned to tie your shoes? And your best friend in kindergarten brought candy to school and said you could have whatever you choose. Then you were fifteen at a crossroad with names scribbled in a journal and you were confused because you had a crush on a girl in your class but you were scared it showed. Then you asked your teachers if there were any proper way to describe a love story but they told you it's not a feeling you learn in school. So you taught yourself and you began to understand the things that made you feel like you were little again, and that love was as simple as tying your shoes.

Most nights, the home that is meant to keep you safe feels like a minefield of dangerous conversations and forgotten memories. I know that the dark feels better, underneath the covers where you can block out the shouting. I am sorry that your safe haven tries to ignore who you are and it feels like you are drowning. All the times they tell you it's a phase and the name-calling sends your mind into a daily haze. I am sorry they are stitched so tightly together they may never be opened. But you keep holding on, and one day you will be free.

If I could protect you
from all the things they'll say
I would
If I could tell you
it gets better before the storm
then you'd be misinformed
But I can tell you that
you are doing just fine
because who you are
is important
and I know you'll shine

I know it hurts. The name-calling and the abuse from strange people who don't even know you. Don't let them have your energy. You are not a disgrace, abomination, or accessory. You are a lion who lives among a flock of cowards. Take those words and bury them in the soil. Speak kindly to them so that they will not rot, but instead grow empathy in its place. It is easy to want them to suffer, but believe me, when they fill spaces with hate, they are already suffering.

I want to tell you the world is at your feet and not to hide away each day and week after week. But I can't promise that things will be easy. I can't promise some days won't be hard. I wish I could protect you from all the opinions out there. About why you shouldn't be this way or how your love is wrong. But I can't. I can't protect you from these things any more than I can protect myself. But I can give you these words, as many as I can. To sometimes read or sit somewhere on your shelf. And I can promise you that no matter where you go in life or however people try to denounce who you are, you are a miracle and a fighter.

Darling, you were born from a star.

And his father said
two boys should never kiss
But the boy had a lover whose eyes
reminded him of a velvet sky
The boy had a lover whose voice
called out his forgotten name
Until one day the boy said
I'll kiss you later
but later never came

I wanted to pull you down between my thighs and blanket myself with you. Your hair on my face and how you smell like honey in the way you do. I wanted to kiss every curve and touch all the parts of your skin. I wanted to make you forget the places others have been. I just wanted to show you that I love you more than anything.

Sometimes people will tell you that you're too young to know what you want. They will make you feel like you can't talk about the person you love because your love isn't right. You might change the pronouns in the things you write or feel scared when the line in a song means something different to you. And so you will live inside a closet with your dreams and your hopes because it feels like someone is on the outside, holding it firmly shut. I just wanted to let you know that it isn't all lonely. When you're ready to open the door, we'll be on the other side with a welcome party.

I am learning to press love into my skin
instead of opening old wounds
and letting all the angry energy in
I am finding light in this reckoning
dusting my bones from this painful ash
I am no more in denial
about who I ought to be
than the universe is of all its stars
when the comet begged to be free

The first time we kissed, the sun was low and the air had filled with daisies, and I remember wondering if the earth had become more beautiful or if your perfume was clouding all my insecurities and hidden maybes. When you said my name, you sounded so far away, like the words had been held for such a long time, and you were calling me home, back to a place I once belonged. I was scared to want more because the night air had covered our faces and crowds were trickling into the streets. But I couldn't see any others, only you in your white dress and worn-out sneakers. I wanted to know you better, learn to love you in every season. Because all the years I'd been scared about what people may say, you had suddenly become all my reasons.

We spend the early hours of the morning planning our future between cups of coffee and toast smeared with butter. We think about what our children will look like and if we'll have a dog or a cat or both. Even if I tried, I could never change how I feel about her. She is my morning sunrise, sleepy eyes that remind me forever exists and a home is nothing more than a goodnight kiss and an arm around my waist in the middle of the night. Someone reminded me the other day that people still stare. Their brows crease, wondering why we are holding hands or why I lean in to kiss her lips on the escalator. Small children pause in their thinking, speculating whether two women are meant to be in love. But they say each year brings new change, so I will have hope. Maybe next year we will be in Paris or London, maybe even Rome. A few years after that, I hope we come home and people won't stare so much. It's your choice, they will say. It has nothing to do with me and everything to do with you and her. I hope we have a family one day, with stars in their eyes and nothing but love in their hearts. Maybe even grandchildren, and they'll laugh and write poems about how silly the old days used to be. Yet if nothing changes and people still stare and our home still holds onto all its fears, it's not going to change how I feel about her. How she lights up even the darkest of days. Because even if I had nine lives, and you still refused our rights, I would spend each one loving her.

My soul has been unearthed
from deep within the soil
And my bones feel
like ashes
charred, empty, spoiled
We have marched forward
toward light and love
And yet we are still met
with picket lines and politics
with angry words and ways too deeply set
And in the night I reach for her
she keeps me safe
My other half to help carry this weight
just a reminder
our love should not be a debate

Love is the space between your dreams
where anger and hatred are not allowed
and the closet does not exist
So with every breath
it is the ignorance we will resist

THE
SKY

There is nothing
a sky full of stars cannot teach
a conversation in moonlight
a sunset on a deserted beach
You are capable of anything
Keep your goals in sight

In late September
I was on your roof
my feet held high in the air
thinking about how everything
in life isn't always fair
But I feel safe in your arms
knowing I've found a love
that feels like a sunrise

Behind my eyes is a galaxy of swirling stars
and a sky that changes with the weather
And I'm begging the world to come back
to its roots
I'm dreaming of the day we can all exist together
      in peace

In a field where wildflowers grow
I hoped to find you staring into the sunlight
dipped in yellow

On the road
with guitar strings
and campfires
holding hands
and looking at the moon
I'd spend the rest of my life falling in love with you

The world has been unkind today
        she said
        So I replied
Step into my arms
        And with my chin upon her head
        I whispered
Let me be kind instead

I have been afraid, because there were days when I did not know who I was without loving you. But in the dawn, the mist rolls onto my lawn, and I will keep going, even if the healing takes weeks and weeks.

The night is dotted with stars
and I imagine them as fireflies of hope
blanketing the earth

She reminded me of a ballerina in a snow globe
not because she was fragile
No
But because each time the music played and she would dance
my eyes couldn't look away

Self-worth is very strange
We spend hours convincing others to have it
And not enough time convincing ourselves

Often I have wondered in a crowded room
if each person represented the love I had for myself

how crowded the room would be

In the cover of night, I took a ladder and made my way into town. And underneath the moon I stood and watched the ladder reach into the stars. I climbed each rung, my heart in my chest, my dreams floating before me. Until I was looking over a city blinking in the dark, with lights stretched as far as the sea. I moved further than I thought I could. I felt the pull of the sky, the call of the wild. A lavender blue with a circle light, reminding me all my dreams were valid, the first step was just to take flight.

The colors bled from her
in orange and pink and yellow
Tears the shapes of clouds
a sunrise, bright and loud
because she loved her more than the sky

And she wondered if pain was laced with gold
how many people would want it

Festival

soft words and gentle hearts
kind eyes and forgotten souls
long journeys and new starts
rain dances and no control

To love another without selfishness is the highest act of love

Just because you don't fight fire with fire, doesn't mean you are weak. Sometimes choosing to be the bigger person takes more courage than giving in to the bitter words we so often speak. There can be power in silence. If you choose to take the high road, you are not a coward. A plane can still be heard, even behind the clouds.

Be your own pilot.

When you are little, the storm seems like the sky is angry. Like every cloud screams with each clap of thunder. But you grow older and sometimes screaming is the only thing you feel like doing.

Your mother tells you that
you are a flower
Yet you are wondering
why you have not been picked
But here is a reminder:
the garden has never looked so beautiful

It was late at night
and bedtime had come too soon
but the little girl seemed curious
Please leave the curtains open
      she said
I need to see the moon

I know that everyone talks about fireflies. They talk about stars in the sky and comets streaking by. They say how pretty the sun looks after the rain and the way grass feels under bare feet. They dress up the pretty things in life but they dress down the 'ugly' things. But I want to dress up all things. That seems fair.

Sometimes you choose to never speak to someone again. That someone could be an old lover or an old friend. It's not because you are bitter or angry. It's not because you haven't forgiven. It's because you haven't forgotten. How they tried to take away the best parts of you. Surviving someone is enough reason to remove them from your life.

What holds meaning to another may not hold meaning to you. But this doesn't make it any less valid. Allow people to talk about what is important to them.

It is good for the soul.

They do not complete you
You are more than a half
You are the whole picture

There is beauty in discovering who you are. It fills you up in the same way the sun fills the sky on a summer day. You don't have to be in love to love yourself.

You forget what the pain feels like until it comes around again. But you remember where you were and what you were doing when your life seems like it's falling apart. I was on the balcony and you had said let's just be friends. I remember the sky, it had looked so beautiful. And I'd wondered how I could feel so empty when there was beauty all around me.

You don't need to thank someone because
you're hard to love

     They love you because it's hard not to

I think you are infinite
the way you hold yourself
how smart you are
all these stories you have
each bruise and every scar

Hold your own hand. Open your own doors. You are an ocean, a sky, a forest of trees. Don't forget to love yourself and say thank you and please.

They may get angry, you may lose a lover or a friend, but one day wherever they end up, they will thank you for your honesty.

It's not always easy to believe
in yourself
Especially on the days your bones
ache so badly
they feel brittle.
It will feel as though
you will never be strong again
and the road is impossible
to walk.
But these are the days
you need the belief the most.
I hope you find solace in the below
I believe in you

People have given up on small talk. They don't want to talk about the weather or how you wear your hair. They want 3 a.m. conversations under a bright starry night. But I'm asleep at 3 a.m. and I'm dreaming about you and the day we had been talking about the new florist that opened on the corner. I like talking about the weather because the sun reminds me of your hair and the sky reminds me of your eyes. Small things lead to big things, it's just some people want to skip over it. I don't want to miss out on that.

Just because someone else doesn't validate you
doesn't mean you can't validate yourself

THE
SEA

Healing is like being at sea
There are storms and then it is quiet
There are moments of calm
and moments you can't stand
And above anything, it may take a little while
before you see land

The Heartbreaker

If they can justify why they broke your heart, they are not sincere. If they can continuously turn your pain into pain of their own, they are not sincere. Selfish people will find reasons and excuses. They will turn themselves into the victim time and time again because they do not want to take responsibility for the guilt. Someone who is genuinely sorry will never choose whether they hurt you or not. Instead they will accept the pain they caused you, and they will say, "I'm sorry."

The ache doesn't have an expiration date any more than healing has a time limit. You are allowed moments of doubt. You are allowed setbacks.

There is purpose to the pain
and it is not to wish it upon others
Hurting someone else
won't heal the holes in your heart

I came to your garden to watch it grow
  but you set everything alight
and instead I witnessed a wildfire

Some days feel like a bar fight, trapped under the dimly lit ceilings, backed into the stained walls. I'm trying to crawl out. I'm trying not to fall.

It's been such a long winter.
There were moments my chest felt so tight
I wasn't sure if I was still breathing.
But soon the snow will melt away
and the flowers will start to grow again.

Forgiving them won't always stop the ache. When you let someone into your heart and they make a mess, you don't have to keep them in your life. Remove what is toxic. You are better off without it.

You were abusive, and it took me such a long time to recognize all the signs and all the red flags. I was so angry at myself for trusting in someone so cruel. A monster in disguise, a person who lies. But in the end I thanked you for showing me that the illness and the selfishness are not an excuse.

Scars show a journey, but first the wounds need to close.

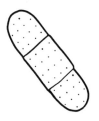

People who love endlessly despite all the hurt are the reason there is light. Do not let anyone try to diminish how big your heart is. It's important you continue to love.

They will try to justify their actions by telling you they can change, but someone who takes pride in breaking someone else's heart isn't someone who is on your side.

The first time she took her clothes off, her dress fell lightly to the floor and I saw all the scars stitched into her skin. I asked her what had happened and she told me the pain had come from within. I wanted her to know that I thought her to be very brave, but my lips to her scars was all I could manage. And the scent of her skin, I wanted to save.

The grief feels like lightning
never striking the same place twice
but rather striking every part of my heart
until it's shattered in so many pieces
        I am unsure how to gather them all again

Even pain must wonder why it has a role to play

Someone once told me that the art of healing lies in how many times you can stop yourself from crying. But I think it's more than that; I think it's how hard you can cry and still know you'll be okay in the morning.

I looked at her
and told her she was worth
all the struggle
in all that life made us do
And when she looked
back at me
she told me
I was worth the struggle too

In February she sat on the balcony with a notebook and her tea
and she wrote everything down about feeling alive again
and what it's like just to be

Tell your daughter she is loved
Tell her she can do anything
Tell her there is power in her mistakes
and even more in her learning

When you laugh, it starts in your soul and ripples all through your bones. It fills all the spaces that were once so hollow.

Laugh plenty, laugh often.

But sometimes it's not about changing
it's about accepting that not all things can be changed

How to Feel

Cry in the shower and then take a long walk. Sing in the car and at the supermarket. Ask a stranger for the time even if you are shy. Drive with the windows down and the wind in your hair. Watch the sun rise over your city. Fold paper cranes and write love notes. Tell someone to have a good day. Notice the sky and the sun and the trees. Remind yourself that you are worth more than you've ever been able to see.

If you imagine yourself as a vessel, moving through the motions of life, you can imagine that you will need care and repair. Not every day will be pleasant. There is going to be thunder and lightning. But you are magnificent and you carry yourself with grace, with each stroke you need to keep moving, back to your safe place.

I hope the peace will come
You deserve it

You can't hide the things that lay deep within your soul. They become a part of you. They are your journey, the other side to your whole.

Little bursts of jealousy are good sometimes. They keep you driven, keep you motivated. They're like small flowers seeing tall flowers and wanting to grow a little more. But don't dwell on jealousy; it'll make you cruel and you'll eventually wilt.

Everybody wants to feel special, like they are different and unique. But you are born a tiny spark in an awfully large universe. You are already an atom that makes the world different. You are already needed for its balance.

There is a longing when you are apart from the one you love.
It is a pain found in each mile the distance leaves.
It stays with you, weighs so heavy on your chest,
some days it's hard to breathe.

You are not weak in those quiet moments you have to yourself. All the pain you carry inside you will be stardust soon, for you to store upon your shelf.

The world is a constellation
and even if sometimes you see yourself
      as a tiny star
you are a link that makes the universe
      turn over
It would not be the same without you

But constant validation is not a good thing.
You are not always going to win.
You are not always deserving of the prize.
It's important to stay humble.
A hunger to improve is powerful.

When you look at your body and you believe it to be an anchor that weighs you down, the ship will not sail. But if you fill your body with breaths of fresh air and remind yourself anchors can be lifted, you'll become the ocean.

Healing isn't always soft. It can be loud and come in waves of angry tears. It won't always follow your rules, and on some days it may even bring out your deepest fears. It will feel like things are falling apart and the world sees you as a ghost. You will beg your house to burn down with you in it, just to stop feeling so lost. But beneath each breath is a small new start. A tiny margin of hope, when it feels like the healing becomes further and further apart. Because on each day you take a breath and admire all your rough edges, you step closer to realizing that there is no right or wrong in your healing. The hope will grow, your strength will sprout, and you will understand there is validation to your feelings.

THE
ROAD

Journeys are not all the same
Some take longer than others
Some are gray and some are filled with colors
In the end it's not nearly about
the difficulty or the forgotten days
It's about you
and what you learned along the way

The further you go, the more days you win.
Even on the bad days, you are still getting through them.

And I told you to take care
and I wished you all the best
Thinking maybe you'd come back
once you were done with all the rest
But I moved on and found someone new
and in case you didn't know
I'm happier without you

My shadow seems tired
We are separated when we should be united,
And I ask if there is anything I can do
But my shadow replies,
I am tired of being you

The Other Side of Sad

It's not like you wake up one day and all the pain is gone. It's more like each day the ache moves over and there is a little more space to give to happiness and laughter and sunshine.

Don't make a mess of someone else's heart just because you are trying to figure out yours. Tell them from the start: I don't know what I want, so make sure you protect your heart.

The River and the Sea

There is a river and she runs through the land
and out into the open sea
She dances wildly around a bank of evergreen trees
and slows down before the bend
She knows there is joy in the journey
and that all things must come to an end

Abuse is as terrible as it sounds. If you have never been abused, then you have no right to tell a victim how they should rebuild their strength or how they should fight back. If they want to cry or get angry, let them. You have to let someone come back to themselves. You have to let them grieve the person they left behind. It's not your choice to say how or when.

Above me the clouds are rolling in
and they are of all the places I have ever been
The air is cool and soft
and I can't wait to come home

People don't notice the things they no longer care for. If they cannot text you back or take interest in your life, it is because you are one of the things they no longer notice. You deserve to be in the spotlight, so stop wasting your time on people who no longer care.

Ready

When I look at her, I see a life I've never seen before. In the car listening to songs we both know the words to. In the store finding cheap bottles of wine for a party we were both invited to. Holding hands over dinner, in a restaurant where the waiters whisper they know we're in love. There are no more lonely nights, thinking about the kind of love I deserve. Instead there are days filled with things that feel right and kisses that reach every nerve. She is that feeling that feels right, and I know I'm ready to settle down with her.

That heart of yours may feel delicate at times
especially when someone creates holes it never asked for
But don't deny it the chance to love again
never be ashamed to love harder than the love before

You don't get to choose how other people love. If someone wants to fall in love after two weeks, then let them. If someone wants to fall in love after three months, a year, never, whatever: let them. People are always trying to make decisions for other people.

Focus on your own.

Motions

You know, I think we'd get along. Not because we have anything in common (unless you like half moons, turtles, and the way your garden smells after the rain) but because I'm going through the motions, too. Day by day, week by week. Some are good, others are bad, every so often some are horrible. But we just keep going, you know. We try to make sense of the things around us, wonder if we are speaking too loud or not enough. We wonder if we have impacted anyone's lives yet or if anyone is going to impact ours. We think about heartbreak and love and paying the bills. We're just people going through the motions.

Strangers but friends at the same time.

People will surprise you with their sensitivity. The hardest of people could be the ones who crumble in your arms. Try not to assume on first glance.

Be gentle.

Shared memories are remembered differently
It means something to you but means
something different to them
Blame changes the stories on both sides

It's not your responsibility to be the foothold as someone else grows up. If you know where you are or what you want, don't apologize for not being interested in people who don't. At the same time, don't blame someone for growing—you were there once, too.

But all things start and end with ourselves.

They don't deserve you if they try to diminish your goals and dreams. They don't deserve you if they tell you to be quiet when you are talking about your passions. They don't deserve you if you have to justify your personal space and your need to be an individual. Relationships are not meant to be a cage. You are meant to work as a team. If your teammate isn't running with you, then don't bother with the marathon.

There was a forest beyond the rolling hills, and in the winter it was burned to the ground. It was damaged so badly nothing was left, not even a sound. But from the ashes, new trees began to grow, and the river began to run, and the flowers sprouted in new rows. The forest reminds me of you, how you took back what was yours. And reminded the world you survived all these horrible wars.

One day you will wake up and the day ahead won't be filled with such dread. You'll make yourself some coffee and put on your shoes and things will be better than they are now.

If you are selfish for the wrong reasons, and you do not give, a poison will grow inside you. It will run so deep in your veins you will forget what it means to love a stranger as your sister or brother.

All of us can be insecure. There are no rules as to how much or how little.

> But I don't think your body takes up too much space
>> because the spaces that you fill deserve to
>> be explored.

There is nothing wrong with your laugh.

> A loud laugh can be heard for miles;
>> happiness deserves to travel.

I don't care if you send long messages or talk about your dreams.

> I want to hear about them.

Stop apologizing for not being the things you think someone wants you to be.

> That is not your responsibility.
>> It's their responsibility to love these things
>> about you.

If you could separate yourself from your soul—what would you say?

Would you take your soul in your arms and ask if it was doing okay?

And if your soul said no and it wanted to be held, would you hold your soul in your arms and be a little kinder?

Would you plant validation in the places that have gone dark?

Would you remind your soul it mattered?

> I hope you would speak soft words and let the flowers grow again.

Hold on to the ones who notice.
They are usually the people who ask
     Are you okay
Even when you've spent the whole night pretending.

Your whole life is about learning. You're not going to get to the point where you know all there is to know. That's the exciting part. You get to live each day discovering something new.

Sometimes it's difficult to be nice to others
not because we don't want to
but because they're not easy to be good to

As you get older, your body will change. You will have stretch marks and wrinkles, gray hairs and cellulite. But it's never about the way a castle ages. It's about how the castle makes you feel when you walk inside and the lanterns are still bright.

Even good people make mistakes. Sometimes, you have to let people be young and forge their own paths.

The doubt will creep up on you. It will start with how you do your hair and even what you have chosen to wear. It will turn you inside out and make you think there are things holding you back. But if you are reading this: the only person doing that is you.

You don't have to apologize for wanting something for yourself. You spend all your days being a stepping-stone to other people's success. Sometimes you just have to walk away and let them make it on their own.

But you have to take care of yourself. Eat well, keep moving, talk about your feelings. There are bad days, but they don't dismiss the good in all your healing.

You are going to change directions. You will choose the wrong path hundreds of times before you choose the one that makes sense. It's never about the end. The road is always about the twists, the turns, and the bends.

THE
MOUNTAINS

There will be times when the mountain feels too great
And your days are filled with less love and a little more hate
But the point is to always keep climbing
For even the bravest are sometimes scared to reach
And the wisest have trouble in what to teach
But with deep breaths and a nod to the sky
You can reach the top of even the tallest mountains
Just ignore any soul that ever tells you not to try

Grow gracefully
Even if you make mistakes
Even if there are storms
Grow in the day
Grow in the night
Grow into yourself
Love your light

Lanterns

Along the pathway, may lanterns light as you pass. Filled with magic, may you bloom with dignity and class. With every breath, may flowers grow from the dust. May you find courage in your growth, because you deserve freedom and peace, if not both.

It will not break you. Dust yourself off, take a step forward, don't let them see you despair. You are more than a ghost on a lost highway. You are the morning, the river, every breath of fresh air.

Some will tell you not to be a sad person. They will encourage you to be happy, without realizing happiness is sometimes the greatest challenge. They will remind you that a sad life is not a life lived.

But sadness is not a curse.
It will not end you.
Your life still has meaning, even if sadness plays a large part.

Just remember if sadness has room in your heart, so does happiness.

And if magic exists
It's because it exists in you
How you hold yourself
in times of trouble
How you light up each
and every room
You may tread carefully sometimes
but always remember
the most beautiful flower
takes its time to bloom

There will always be people who call you names and mock your art. Sometimes those things won't even phase you. Other times, they'll sink so deep into your veins you feel like you might choke on the ache they cause. But those who use words to create pain or spread hatred do not understand how to use them. They throw them around carelessly, foolishly. They beg you for attention because they want so desperately for you to notice. Ignore these people. Use your words to encourage, seek, and spread love.

You are allowed to outgrow someone. If the river parts ways, you can forge your own path to the sea.

Everybody gets lost
and it is hard to come home again
It's like saying to your soul
I want to find you
But neither of you know
where to start

I'm sure there are things better left unsaid
and feelings better left alone.
But if you do not speak,
and you do not feel,
then how can you possibly move on?

We were in a coffee shop
Life and I
We were thinking about the things ahead
and watching the cars go by
And I asked Life if I was going to be happy
if I was going to be served well
And at first Life didn't answer
and the silence brewed between us
So I asked again
will everything work out, Life?
will I have love and faith and trust?
And then Life nodded and said
you will, but first you must learn
that struggle makes you strong
and while pain may hurt and burn
you will need these things to live
you will need them to live long

Sometimes words are the last thing you need
Instead you just need silence and a cup of tea

Mother

I had a bouquet of dreams and I tossed them in the air, and they landed in the arms of my mother. And she looked at me and said, "Darling, you'll need these." So I began to take back my dreams, one after the other.

There is no advice on this page
only love
      and acceptance
           and that I am proud of you

Before I leave this life, I want someone to feel safe with me. With every bad day, heartache, and misery. I want them to be able to crawl into my arms in the middle of the night and be reminded that someone in the world loves them with every breath.

She held all her magic in the palm of her hand, wondering, if light could be carried in veins, would the universe finally understand?

What do you do when you can no longer exist beside yourself?

You open some windows
lie down in the middle of your floor
and remember you can win this war

Things your heart wants you to Know

Take care of yourself
Drink water
Watch the clouds go by
Cry when you need to cry
Smile at yourself in the mirror
Only you validate you
To be beautiful is to be kind
Remind yourself to try
Your mistakes do not define you

To be known for kindness and everlasting light. To be known for strength and courage and all things bright. To be full of mercy and selflessness. That is beauty.

There was a child with sunflowers in her hand
and she wondered if when she grew up
she would have all the same rights as a man
because her father loved her so
and her brother was kind
But she soon learned
not all are of the same mind
but she carried on and she found her way
spending all her days and hours
spreading happiness with sunflowers

You will go through life as a continuous cycle of change. You are the wind that folds and glides. The sea that turns with the tide. Every new beginning demands a different version of you. Make each one better than before.

We love, we laugh, we cry, and we break.
We plan, we wish, we take risks.
And we do all this until our last breath.
            Cherish each moment.

You have these moments when nothing is going your way.
Every little catastrophe, every little reason to say,
I've had enough of me.
It won't feel like your week, your month, your year.
You'll come home most nights and burst into tears.
But you are an adventure, of lost maps and highways.
And if anyone can lead the way,
It's you.

Bonsai trees are small trees grown from bigger trees. All the fine details, from the branches to the leaves. Even the smallest of dreams have meaning.

If you are not sure whether you are in love because of them or in love because you are lonely, head to the mountains and take in the world. Be reminded that you will always have yourself.

You keep growing. Even when you are in a relationship, your branches are still growing, and little buds start blossoming. It's just some people grow in opposite directions, others grow beside each other, and some grow entwined.

Self-love is taking a deep breath before bed and promising to rise again tomorrow

You are not defined by the stage you are at in life. Just because you are unsure of where you are heading doesn't mean you don't know who you are inside.

The peace starts in your mind and travels through your veins and into your heart. It becomes your body, your soul, your home. After all the years of aching, the relief feels like it could move mountains.

She doesn't open up easily and she has high walls. Cautious about leaping into arms that won't catch her if she falls. She gives plenty, more than enough. But sometimes in the early hours she comes undone.

The hurt will go.

When it came it settled itself into your heart and occupied most of your thoughts. It chose to stay and turned your stomach into knots. And while it may take some time, eventually it will pack up and leave.

The hurt feels heavy now, but it will go.

It will make sense one day. Why some things happen and why others don't. You've been hurt probably more than you deserve. But the hurt is worth staying alive for. Because you'll live to see the day that shows you all things pass.

Some chapters will be harder to read than others. You'll feel like every word aches, like every page must burn. But there are steps between every line, and no matter the distance, you have to continue to climb.

THE
FIELDS

We are together in these open fields
Our colors
Our wants
Our hopes and dreams
Even on nights we struggle
We are together

Today I sat on a hill with daisies and I asked them to teach me how to open up. And then I walked beside roses hoping they'd teach me how to bloom. Because most days I am a lonely tree, with roots so deep below the soil I am unsure how to let go.

I will never apologize for using soft words. I will never apologize for being gentle with other hearts. I will never apologize for laughing at things that may seem silly or for being a little strange some days. The world can be a dark and unforgiving place, so I look to the light.

I've been pretending, and in my dreams, I am running into your open arms. But I can't make you love me. It's dark outside, but if I close my eyes, I can see you slipping away. Morning will come and I'll give up my heart. Because when the sun rises, you'll be gone.

On a flight, sitting in the window seat. I'm staring at the clouds. All the thoughts inside have lately been so loud. Where I'm headed, even I don't know. I wish I were a bird with open wings, and I could stay up in the sky.

I'm trying to forget how I ended up on this road
where our love suddenly became
you, me, and the other.

Well, we gave it our all. But somewhere our love got caught in the middle. Late at night, she's pouring her soul out over the phone, but I'm not on the other end.

The Goodbye Book

If you had a goodbye book, how long would the pages be? Would there be apologies or angry letters or blank spaces full of missed opportunities? Would you cry when you read it or turn the pages over quickly? Would you hold it in your arms or bury it under your bed? If you had a goodbye book, how many names would it have?

Poetry shouldn't be confined to a single definition
It is expression
Each person expresses things differently
You don't get to define how someone bleeds
You don't get to choose how someone opens their heart and
splits at the seams

But the actions of one do not represent the actions of all

She must have broken your heart, because I found you on the side of the highway. You were crying an old song that had been sung before. About a boy who loved a girl but then she left. And in the middle of the night you called her phone and recorded voice mails begging her not to leave. But she had already gone, back in April, when she told you it was too hard to go on.

Whenever you're around, I'm rehearsing all the words to say. I'm feeling guilty because I can't stop all the thoughts in my head. And I keep thinking one night you'll change my mind. This was never going to be easy, but some things just never are. I think we are coming to an end.

A young person is not to be belittled or mistreated or left cold and alone.

A young person is to be nurtured, cared for, watched over while they grow.

There is power in shaping a future.

Make sure it's done with love and understanding.

There are still gentlemen in the world
They'll hold open a door for the women they love
And they'll cradle their little girls in their arms
And weep

Over the years, my heart grew guarded. Fences were built and the signs politely asked people to keep their distance. I was a solitary castle, hidden deep within the woods. Until one day a girl knocked on the door and I couldn't turn her away. She taught me about life and reminded me of sweet tea on a hot summer's day. So I drew back the curtains and opened the walls, and I told the world I was in love with a girl who had roses in her hair and wore bright blue overalls.

When everyone else told me I was a closed case
you were the first to remind me I was an open book

I'd spend all my days on a blanket by the river, watching her eyes light up over wine. And it kills me whenever we're apart. Because she's the only love I'll ever want to know. I haven't felt safe in so long and our future is knocking on my door. I've found a woman to marry and have my children. And what I really mean to say is, she is all the peace I've been hoping to find.

You are in love
when the things you see and the places you go
don't have the same meaning
unless you are sharing them with her.

I fell for you the way leaves do in the fall. I fell for you the way rain does on a cloudy day. I fell for you like snow falls in the winter. But each time you hold me, I forget all the things I wanted to say.

Love can be quiet or loud in diverse and exciting ways. But I wish to write about the love I have for you. How beautiful it is, to live a lifetime knowing your soul is enough for another's. To know there is nothing else they need other than your hand in theirs and your heart on their sleeve.

She was barefoot in our backyard
the grass between her toes
And I'd hoped my heart
would be the only one
she ever knows

An Open Letter to Mum and Dad

Dear Mum and Dad,

There are days I do not say how much I love you, but I am always thinking it. There are days I do not thank you for all the things you have done for me, but I am thinking it. In the times I have needed parents, you have been my parents. In the times I needed friends, you have been my greatest friends. Where there is love and there is kindness, I think of you. Where there is strength and where there is guidance, I think of you. Thank you for bringing me into this life, thank you for loving me as a person. Thank you for chasing my dreams alongside me. When I have children, I will give them the same message: be whomever you want to be.

Love,
Your Daughter

Before you go to sleep
you will think about all the miles you have to go.
And while you dream, I will whisper how proud I am of you
more than you'll ever know.

You'll break before the walls burn
         and your open heart
takes in all the wisdom there is to learn

There will be times happiness hides, and your sadness will feel constant. But it doesn't mean this is all that is left, all that you will do. Sometimes sadness just needs a friend, too.

You're always going to experience negativity from someone. You can't control that. What you can control is how you react to it. The thing is, happy and positive people don't have time to say negative things to people they don't know
because they're too busy being, well,

     happy and positive.

If it doesn't feel right
if it's not what you want
or if you're not ready
then you don't have to love

The most powerful thing I have learned is that no one can hurt you with words. It is you who derives the feelings from the words said. Sometimes the best defense is silence. Don't let those words in. Keep them hanging in the air until they fade away into nothing. Because nothing is going to strip you of who you are and what you deserve.

Your mind is a story that deserves to be read
Your body is a universe that demands respect
Your soul is a song that deserves to be heard

In the open fields
dandelions grow
and you sit among them
hoping your fears will seep into the soil
hoping your dreams will rise into the sky

In the end, life is meant for ups and downs. Your shoes will get muddy, your hair messy in the rain. Afternoons were meant for karaoke and building paper planes.

In your life there will be moments of joy and moments of sorrow. Some days you may not even look forward to tomorrow. You will grow and relish in small things, like shadow puppets on the wall, french fries dipped in ice cream, a small child's smile as they sing. You will be faced with choices, some more defining than others. But the most important thing you can do is to leave your heart open.

To lose, win, and forgive
is simply to live.

THE
HOME

Lately the road has felt long. There were times I could not hear the

things calling me back home. But I'm here now and I feel less alone.

Because in the moments I thought I could not go on, I thought of you.

And how your love kept me going, more than I ever think you will know.

In you,
I see my home, my life, my day's end
listening to your voice in the dark
You are my diary, my love, my other half.

We're young and our hands tremble when we touch, early mornings in the sheets stumbling into skin as our lips meet and you let me in. There are pockets of sunlight seeping in through the windows and with every breath I feel my heart still. Your eyes are every shade of green and in the light sometimes look blue. You whisper my name and it sounds like dreams coming true. We float on a bed that looks like a stormy night and my love for you has been the only thing I've done right.

There are many things I want to do in this life. Like build a tree house, climb a mountain, and call you my wife.

I woke up early this morning. I know that each day of the week you leave before I am barely awake, but today I felt your body turn from the sheets and move about the room quietly. But I kept my eyes closed and I only stirred when you pressed your lips to mine, a goodbye for the day, until you come back home. During the day, I thought about that kiss and I heard some sad stories on the news. And my heart grew heavy for a while because I don't know what I would do if I never got to kiss you again, or hear your laugh, or see that sleepy smile. I wanted to restart the morning. I'd pull back the covers and kiss you until you had to leave. More than anything I want you to know that I cherish every moment, every kiss, and every tiptoe across the room. I love you when the clouds rain, I love you when the night falls, I love you when the flowers bloom, even if in the early morning my eyes are closed.

Sometimes I feel like all my atoms exist just to love you

I love a woman who cares passionately for things. A woman who cares about people and places and what life can bring. I love a woman who makes me better than I was the day before. A woman who every day makes me love her even more.

She came home today with the weight of the world on her shoulders, because this is what life feels like when you get a little older. She started to cry, and I felt my heart ache, because I feel her tears in my soul, they fold and they break. She told me lately she's been scared about finding her purpose in each day. So I put my arms around her and asked her to listen carefully to what I had to say. I told her life is not meant to be easy, and things won't always go our way, but our purpose still remains, even after our hardest day. And I wanted to remind her that she was strong and brave and true, so I told her if anyone can achieve greatness, it's you.

I can't wait to see you again
To tell you all the things I haven't in a while
Like: I love the way your hair falls down your back
And the way you laugh
it reminds me of a song
I love your strength and your bravery
In a world that tries to diminish your dreams
I can't wait to see you again
So the nights won't feel so long

Love isn't about sometimes. You don't get to choose when she needs you. But if you love her, you need to show up when she does.

We all want that. When you feel you have a purpose in someone's life. Even if that purpose is to make toasted sandwiches on a Friday night or listen when she talks about her day. When you are holding her because she's sad and you can feel yourself hugging the sadness away, and there is nothing that will make you move or turn around until the tears are dry and she says she's okay. You go to sleep thinking that if tomorrow comes and you cannot kiss her, every other kiss wasn't enough. Each day the curve of her lips and the way her hair falls down her back makes you wonder if there is anything more beautiful. Then you are reminded of all the small details, like both your toothbrushes sitting side by side on the sink, walking the dog as the day is fading away, and dreaming about the things we forget as we grow older. And you feel at peace because there is nothing more out there. Even though the world will try to convince you that the grass is always greener, you know deep in your heart that it is already green over here. You see it every day, in her.

Pulse

I don't remember what time it was, but it was late and she had fallen asleep, exhausted from the day. I had curled into her, pressed my face into the curve of her neck, and she smelled the way she always does, of sweetness and flowers and all the beautiful things in life. I felt her pulse against my lips as they rested there, connected to each beat as it found its way through her body. I remember thinking it was so strange at first, to feel her pulse against my lips because it was so loud, and it drowned out any other feeling in that moment. It was just the beat of her heart on my lips. Then I started to think about this life that I had crawled up next to and how important it was in my own life. Then I thought about the woman this life belonged to, with her scent of flowers and her pulse beating against my lips, and I realized just how much I loved this woman and how much I valued her life and our life together. So I promised that my lips would speak only kindness to her, that they wouldn't dare kiss anyone else, and if anybody ever hurt her, my lips would comfort her. It was late and I felt her pulse against my lips and it reminded me of how much I loved the woman the pulse belonged to.

It's not about calling her beautiful. It's how you say it. When you call her beautiful, you are pulling every word she is into one: smart, funny, shy, confident, curvy, tall, small, inspiring, strong, kind, and every other thing you love about her. You cannot call her beautiful unless you say it in a way that makes her feel like she can do anything. You cannot call her beautiful unless you say it like it's the last thing you will ever say.

Some people think love is just a figment of another's imagination. That romance has been forgotten and didn't make it to this decade. But I still believe in it. So I hope you find someone who plays with your hair when you're sad, who makes you laugh until your sides hurt, someone who doesn't play games and isn't afraid to say I love you even if it's more than once a day. I hope you find someone who brings toothpaste home because you ran out that morning.

My heart belongs to a woman
faithful and strong and bold
her hand is the only one I hold
And if I had any say
about the way every day goes
I'd spend each one
with her
Because she's the only one who knows
all my hopes, my dreams, my fears
I've found someone who has
made me believe in love everlasting
even after all these years

I was made to keep you safe
So baby let's be brave
Because we're falling more in love

We are never going to agree
on all the same things
And life will get a little crazy
even sometimes a little unhinged
But for all the beautiful moments
and the ones that make us try
I will continue to always love you
even after the day I die

But the sun does not apologize for the days it hides behind the clouds. You are allowed to sleep in and settle under the covers. You are allowed to have moments when life feels like it's standing still. In these moments, rest, recharge, try not to compare yourself to others.

Lately I have been thinking about who I want to be and why I want to move through life better than I was before. I've been thinking about the courage it takes to admit your mistakes and how lonely it feels when your side is not on the side of fate. I've been thinking about growing older and all the responsibility that awaits. I've been thinking about sharing secrets and dreams, watching sunsets in solitude, packing suitcases and boarding planes and what it all means. Lately I've been thinking about following the lighthouse home, coming back to the parts of me I lost, when I wasn't so afraid and my heart was soft.

The unknown is feared the most
Some dread it so much it makes their edges rough
But there is beauty in not knowing
and adventure
To dive into yourself and discover the part you have yet to meet
Is an adventure worth living

When your heart awakens
and crawls out of bed
just remember to give it joy
let it race
and remind it that home
is never far away

Writing about you isn't always easy. Sometimes I feel guilty, because there aren't enough words to describe how much I love you.

I knew I loved you before you even said a word. Maybe we have been planned all along, but in a crowded room, all other faces are blurred. There are some things you just don't question, but before you, I learned all my lessons. And I've lost my heart because now it's all yours. I've waited my whole life to find you.

If our bed were a canvas
Then our colors
Would bleed into each other
In the way
Paint creates art

I'd always been insecure about my glasses
and the freckles across my nose
I'd never had any faith in the things I do
Until I met you
and you showed me that I was beautiful
and that all my thoughts mattered
You reminded me that all my parts could heal
even if some had shattered
So I wanted to thank you
For bringing out the best in me
and loving the parts no one else can see

It was the weekend and we had been asleep until noon, and I'd watched you get dressed in the early afternoon. You begged me to see a movie, and I said okay, even though it was a film I probably wouldn't normally see. I remember in the theater, with our popcorn and our soda, your hand in my hand and my arm draped over your shoulder: I watched you instead. I counted the scenes that made you laugh and the ones that made you cry. If you were a cinema, I knew only the best pictures would play. And no matter where you were or what you were doing, I could watch you all day.

I'd cross oceans and highways and meet every struggle for you
But I know you know this already
Because you'd do the same for me too

Our hearts have become involved
A dance we are still trying to learn
But in the corner
under the lights
I would dance with you all night

After all this time, I still can't believe we were once strangers. There was a time in my life that I didn't even know she existed. I didn't know her favorite color, or the songs she loves, or how her lips look in the sunlight. Now we have all these memories together. I love her. I always want to create memories with her.

It's ten years later and I still love the way you laugh. We watch reruns on a Friday night and the world goes by from the coffee shop on the corner. I'm still yours, like the way the night has always loved the moon.

Sometimes I think of your body as a home. It won't matter how many years we have been in love. I know that it's your home and I will always respect that. And while your walls are beautiful and the lights in your eyes are like magic, through the windows I see the heart of the fireplace as it calls my name. To run my hands along those walls and carve my name into the fireplace is a gift I will always treasure.

I've been thinking about you
in moments that never seem to change
because while the world
keeps moving on an enormous stage
you and I are alone
still
in each other's gaze

We had our backs to the ground with the grass stretched out before us. You were wearing a sundress. I remember because it was the one with the blue stitched pattern on the front. The day had been warm, and my lips ached for you, just one last kiss before we were called home by the rainstorm. The clouds began to roll in, slowly at first, one over the other, dotting the sky until they spread farther and farther. I felt your shoulder on my shoulder and your fingers playing with the hem of my shirt, and I remember you asked if I believed in magic. I laughed because I love when you say things like that but you pointed at the clouds and asked if I could see the bear with the hat. It didn't matter how long we lay there, turning clouds into shapes. I just wanted to hear you turn shapes into stories. Then you pointed and told me that one looked like a heart and you asked if you had mine. And I said you did, because I could see your heart more clearly than any of the other clouds combined.

I could press my thumb to each of the freckles on her skin and I could tell her each one is worth an I-love-you. But then I would spend my life counting all her freckles over and over again.

Sometimes it's not about finding someone to love you. It's about recognizing when someone already does.

There have been many times
I have fallen in love
with the wrong person
I have found myself with an ache
as lonely as my empty sheets,
But life is about knowledge
and taking chances
and dancing in the streets,
So when all my roads
ended up at you
I knew life wouldn't be the same,
Because I am in love with
every little thing
like your freckles
your warmth
and how you say my name.

My heart felt like an attic, and I was spending each day breathing dust until the light crept in from the cracks in the walls and I saw her standing by the door. My thoughts settled to the sound of her voice, and my trembling hands had a body to hold. And my love for her grew with every turn and every fold.

Home is sometimes coming back to yourself. When all has been forgotten and you feel lost. It is the moment you realize darkness holds as much beauty as light. When you remember the feeling of bare hands in snow, the first smell of spring, and the importance of letting kind people in. Home is rising to start another day and knowing that despite all things, you will find your way.

See you at home. I'll leave the light on